Ellen Anne Eddy's
Dye Day
Workbook

By Ellen Anne Eddy
Author of *Thread Magic:*
The Enchanted World of
Ellen Anne Eddy

Introduction

Everyone you teach teaches you. The first time I taught someone to dye fabric, she spent a full three hours asking me, "Is this all you do?" It was not a silly question. What I do is not complicated in terms of process or technique. I regularly teach dyeing to small children and let them loose. The techniques I use are transparently simple. But the knowledge behind it is not.

What I really teach adults is an understanding of how colors relate to each other. Dyeing is the ultimate test of our understanding of color theory. This book is set up to help you understand those relationships and to put them into your dyeing and your work.

So get your crayons or colored pencils and join me. I've set this up like a coloring book because I firmly believe that all learning works better if it's through more than one information channel. Different people learn through different ways. Some need to see things, some need to hear things, but almost everyone can take in information from action and touch. So in class, I make people color in the shapes. It's another way to help you internalize the color wheel.

We also need to translate commercial dye names. These are often frustrating, as there is no consistency between companies. But it is essential to be able to identify the colors. So we are stuck with names that fail us, being verbal rather than visual and that aren't always the same. We'll do the best we can. The charts should help translate between the two big dye companies, Dharma Trading Company and PRO Chemical and Dye. All chart colors are only an approximation. I did not list all the colors, just my favorites. Check their web sites for full listings.

Color theory for dyeing is pigment based. This is very different from computer screen colors and the colors used in commercial printing. Don't let it confuse you. These three processes are like comparing apples, oranges and peaches. It just doesn't work.

Ellen

© 2009 *Dye Day Workbook*
by Ellen Anne Eddy
ISBN 0982290187
Thread Magic Studio Press
125 Franklin Street, Porter, IN 46304
219-921-0885

www.ellenanneeddy.com

Photos © 2009 Courtesy of Lynne Clayton

For all those who refuse to be fashion victims.
And for Mary Annis, my friend.

Color: A Wordless Language

olor is very hard for us to talk about because it is not a verbal thing. Color is all in the eye. Words fail us every time. Is that color blue, or gray or lavender? The truth is that colors are always in relationship with each other and that defines who they are. That blue may be lavender or gray in context to the colors around it.

The only way to understand color combinations is to work with them. This is why, before we start dyeing, I want us to have a common experience and vocabulary. In working with the color wheel we can get a sense of how colors respond to each other and how we respond to them.

By starting with a working relationship with colors, we can feel more confident when we stand at the dye table or the cutting table, making the color decisions that are part of good design.

Color theory is the study those relationships. Like every scientific theory, it is a way of looking at a system. It is not foolproof. But it gives us a structure for understanding where colors stand with each other. From there, we can predict the effects those colors will have on us as artists and on those who view our art. Color is emotion made visible. Our color choices give us the vehicle to express ourselves emotionally.

Your colors are saying something. What do you want your colors to say? Are they full of joy or rage or surprise? Do they dance? Do they float? Do they stomp up and down?

Once we comprehend where colors stand in relationship to each other, we can learn to choose the colors that say what we want to say. When we dye our own fabric we have control over our color vocabulary. To do that, we start by understanding the color wheel.

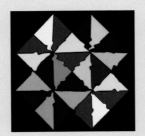

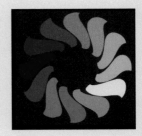

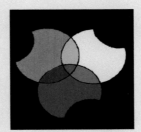

Elements of Color: Hues

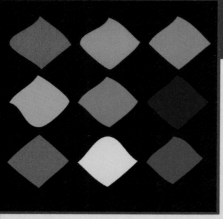

H ues are the actual colors themselves. They are the building blocks of color. We'll first look at the bright jewel tone hues and how they are made. Then we can branch out from tones and tints to neutrals. We'll look at a number of successful color recipes you can use in your own dyeing. Finally, we will tie those colors down to the dye colors produced by the two biggest dye companies in America, PRO Chemical and Dye, and Dharma Trading Company. You'll find their order numbers referenced in the charts, and a more comprehensive dye chart on page 20-21. This way, when you start to order your own dye, you'll be able to do so with confidence.

Primaries

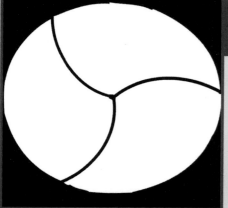

T rue red, blue and yellow are the primary colors. They are the building blocks of the color wheel. They are pure hues and cannot be mixed. Because they cannot be mixed, they stand apart whenever we use them, unless they are part of an analogous color range. They make a strong, solid statement. That is why they're chosen constantly for comic books, children's art and team colors. Color in the primaries: red, yellow and blue.

Primaries	★	★	★
Dharma	2 Bright Yellow	10 Fire Red	22 Cobalt Blue
PRO Chem	104 Golden Yellow	310 N Basic Red	400 Basic Blue

Secondary Colors

The secondary colors are made from mixing primary colors. Orange is a blend of red and yellow. Purple is a mix of red and blue. Green is made from yellow and blue. Because they are mixed colors, they blend in better than primary colors. Still using the red, yellow and blue colors, color in the circles to overlap. Notice what happens to the overlapped colors. Colors we mix are often not as clear and bright as those mixed for us. For that reason, I prefer to work with a large pallet of professionally mixed colors.

Secondaries			
Dharma	6 Deep Orange	18 Deep Purple	66 Kelly Green
PRO Chem	202 Strong Orange	8147 Deep Purple	730 Lime Green

Tertiary Colors

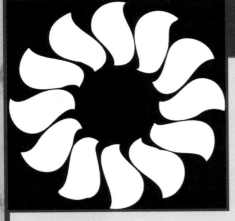

These are the colors in the cracks between the primaries and the secondaries. They are recognizable verbally because they always have double names: Yellow Orange, Red Orange, Blue Green, Yellow Green, Blue Violet, and Red Violet. Tertiaries work and play well with other colors. So they get on with everyone. These are smooth colors that liven everything they touch. Complete the color wheel, adding first the primaries, secondaries and then the tertiaries.

Hint!
There's a full color wheel on the front of the book.

Tertiaries						
Dharma	5 Soft Orange	9 Scarlet	19 Plum	43 Blue Violet	108 Cayman Isle	Not available
PRO Chem	2204 Soft Orange	300 Scarlet	8153 Plum	810 Blue Violet	7132 Cayman Isle	731 Lemon/Lime

Value: Tones

Value is the lightness or darkness of a color. When a color is darkened, we say it is a tone. Tones are darkened or grayed with black, brown or the color's complement. They give us somber, deep shades. Color the whole motif one color. Then color over one section with black, another with brown and third a with the color across the wheel from it, its complement. Notice how different the browns are.

Tones					
Dharma	115 Eggplant	47 Chartreuse	16 Maroon	33 Avocado	N/A
PRO Chem	825 Eggplant	706 Chartreuse	3208 Maroon	7212 Avocado	435 Marine
Dharma	17 Burgundy	15 Amethyst	37 Bronze	32 Olive Drab	111 Black Cherry
PRO Chem	319 Bordeaux	8149 Amethyst	5193 Bronze	7182 Olive Drab	8131 Spicy Plum

Tints

Tints are lightened versions of a color. They can either be paled with white or can be applied lightly. They are airy, delicate and spring-like. Any color can be made into a tint by using very small amounts of dye. Pick three pastels and color the square.

Tints				
Dharma	N/A	48 Robins Egg	61 Ice Blue	7A Peach
PRO Chem	1203 Hollandaise	4143 Robins Egg	4190 Ice Blue	2139 Peach
Dharma	64 Orchid	N/A	12A Baby Pink	60 Lavender
PRO Chem	N/A	331 Cherry Blush	N/A	8133 Lavender

Neutrals

Whites, grays, beiges and browns make up neutral colors. These are colors that have no real color impact. Black and white are are purely themselves. but almost every gray and brown is a tone or a tint exaggerated enough so that all that registers is a neutral hue. Shade this cloud in neutrals.

Neutrals				
Dharma	6A Ecru	42 Charcoal Grey	113 Golden Brown	35A Chocolate
PRO Chem	5223 Ecru	6160 Stormy Grey	1231 Golden Oak	511A Chocolate
Dharma	139 Mist Grey	61 Ice Blue	35 Dark Brown	34 Rust Brown
PRO Chem	6111 Pearl Grey	4190 Ice Blue	510N Basic Brown	5213 Rust Brown

Blacks: The Best Greys

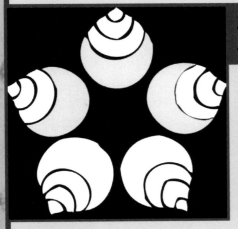

Blacks are a special class in dyeing. It's incredibly hard to dye fabric black. If you need black fabric, you're best off buying it. Instead the best greys come from very weak blacks and other dark tones. Pale New Black has a blue tone; Better Black, purple; Silk Black, greenish; Black, blue green. Jet Black is the darkest black. These greys make great marble colors. Color these pearls in differing shades of grey

Blacks			
Dharma	44 Better Black	300 New Black	39 Black
PRO Chem	N/A	604 New Black	608 Black
Dharma	250 Jet Black	N/A	N/A
PRO Chem	N/A	610 Silk Black	609 Deep Black

Warm and Cool Colors

Colors are classed as either being warm or cool. The cool colors are yellow green, green, blue green, blue , blue violet and purple. The warm colors are red violet, red, red orange, orange, yellow orange, and yellow. Color one fan with warm colors and one fan with cool colors.

Cool						
Warm						

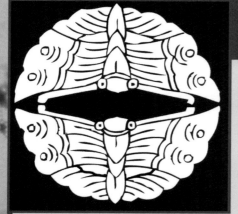

Color Cast: Sun and Shade

Up until now, we have looked at the color through a hypothesis of color theory. It's a valuable tool, but it is just a theory. At a certain point it has to bend a bit to fit reality. We are assuming a perfection that doesn't exist except in theory. If we mix perfect primaries, it should give us clear colors. Experience tells us something different. You can mix yellow and blue and get brown. The colors are not perfect and can lean a little either to the sun or the shade. This is not about being a cool or warm color. It's a color cast. When you look at a color, ask yourself if it is most like the color to the right or the left of it on the color wheel. If the color is more like the one to the right it leans towards the sun. If it's more like the one to the left, it leans towards the shade. You can mix sun colors only or shade colors and be sure of clear hues. If you mix sun and shade, then you get earth. If the color has brown already in it, it's an earth color and anything you mix with it will create more earth. Pages 18-19 have a chart with identifies sun colors(✳), shade colors(☽), and earth colors (✤). Pick colors in the same hue that have one that leans towards the shade and one toward the sun to color these butterflies.

Shade	Colors that lean towards the shade	
	Dharma	**PRO Chem**
☽	13 Fuchsia	308 Fuchsia
☽	19 Plum	8153 Plum
☽	1 Lemon Yellow	114 Lemon Yellow
☽	25 Turquoise	410 Turquoise

Sun	Colors that lean towards the sun	
	Dharma	**PRO Chem**
✳	10 Fire Red	310 N Basic Red
✳	18 Deep Purple	8147 Deep Purple
✳	3A Clear Yellow	1229 Clear Yellow
	22 Cobalt Blue	402C Mixing Blue

Recipes

o far, we've talked about color identity. From here on out, we'll look at the relationship between colors. The combinations made from those connections are my recipes. These are recipes similar to how I cook. I'll use a list of ingredients and go from there. I don't measure, because I do want a unique piece of art from each one of my fabrics. If dyes work as a group, it will work at any strength. Of course you can add or subtract things to your taste. For a sense of what will brown a recipe, check the chart on pages 20-21. You can substitute shade colors with other shade colors, or sun colors with other sun colors, and still get clear hues. If you mix sun and shade or add in earth, you'll get muddy tones.

Monochromatic

A monochromatic color scheme is one that uses one hue in different tints, tones and intensities. These low tension color schemes that are restful. Often monochromatic color schemes mix sun and shade colors to center the colors. These recipes are great for thread, piecing or applique fabric.

Greens	Dharma	PRO Chem
ஐ	92 Bright Green	7158 Bright Green
ஐ	66 Kelly Green	730 Lime
ஐ	31A Forest Green	7195 Forest Green
ஐ	31 Dark green	7207 Dark Green

Reds	Dharma	PRO Chem
✺	9 Scarlet	300 Scarlet
✺	13 Fuchsia	308 Fuchsia
✺	11A Rose Red	305 Mixing Red
✺	10 Fire Red	310N Basic Red

Purples	Dharma	PRO Chem
🌩	64 Orchid	N/A
🌩	18 Deep Purple	8147 Deep Purple
🌩	18A Ultraviolet	8194 Ultraviolet
🌩	19 Plum	8153 Plum

Oranges	Dharma	PRO Chem
○	3A Clear Yellow	1229 Clear Yellow
○	4 Deep Yellow	115 Butterscotch
○	5 Soft Orange	2204 Soft Orange
○	6 Deep Orange	202 Strong Orange

Analogous Colors

Analogous colors are chosen from an arc on the color wheel. These recipes are low tension. They slide into one another, creating harmony. The arc can go as far you would like, using infinite points of shading in between. They make great thread recipes and smooth pretty backgrounds. Pick and color an arc.

	Dharma	PRO Chem
✳	3A Clear Yellow	1229 Clear Yellow
✳	5 Soft Orange	2204 Soft Orange
✳	6 Deep Orange	202 Strong Orange
✳	13 Fuchsia	308 Fuchsia

	Dharma	PRO Chem
◐	80 Robin's Egg	4143 Robin's Egg
◐	25 Turquoise	410 Turquoise
◐	28A Aqua Marine	7140 Aqua Marine
◐	19A Lilac	8199 Lilac

Thermals

The difference in cool and warm color creates a thermal shock reaction. Complementary colors all have that reaction because they are across each other on the wheel. But thermal shock exists in any combination that has cool and warm elements. The shock can either be in hue or in color cast. Sun and shade colors together also give a feeling of thermal shock. Color these leaves in a cool/ warm combination.

	Dharma	PRO Chem
◉	23 Cerulean Blue	406 Intense Blue
◉	10 Fire Red	310 N Basic Red

	Dharma	PRO Chem
◉	13 Fuchsia	308 Fuchsia
◉	6 Deep Orange	202 Strong Orange

	Dharma	PRO Chem
◉	65 Raspberry	8136 Raspberry
◉	28A Aqua Marine	N/A

	Dharma	PRO Chem
◐	3 Golden Yellow	111 Mustard Yellow
	22 Cobalt Blue	402 Mixing Blue

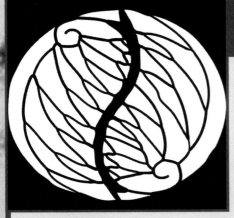

Complementary Colors

 olors opposite of each other on the color wheel are complementary colors. They produce the most amount of tension in electric color schemes. Mixed together they create incredible browns, which resolve the tensions.
Pick a pair and color them as mirror images.

	Dharma	PRO Chem
	9 Scarlet	300 Scarlet
	28A Aqua Marine	N/A

	Dharma	PRO Chem
	N/A	731 Lemon/Lime
	19 Plum	8153 Plum

	Dharma	PRO Chem
	7A Peach	2139 Peach
	80 Robins Egg	4143 Robins Egg

	Dharma	PRO Chem
	10 Fire Red	310 N Basic Red
	30A New Emerald Green	704 Spring Green

	Dharma	PRO Chem
	43 Blue Violet	810 Blue Violet
	3A Clear Yellow	1229 Clear Yellow

	Dharma	PRO Chem
	93 Kilt Green	7218 Kilt Green
	49 Red Wine	312N Strongest Red

	Dharma	PRO Chem
	23 Cerulean Blue	406 Intense Blue
	6 Deep Orange	202 Strong Orange

	Dharma	PRO Chem
	1 Lemon Yellow	114 Lemon Yellow
	19A Lilac	8199 Lilac

	Dharma	PRO Chem
	18 Deep Purple	8147 Deep Purple
	47 Chartreuse	706 Chartreuse

	Dharma	PRO Chem
	14A Hot Pink	3142 Hot Pink
	92 Bright Green	7158 Bright Green

Double Complements

ecipes made from two complements maintain an even stronger tension within them. It's particularly effective if you use complements next to each other.

Color in two complementary pairs together. Overlap them. Watch how the browns mix with each other. These make great nature fabric and thread recipes.

	Dharma	PRO Chem
◈	3A Clear Yellow	1229 Clear Yellow
◈	5 Soft Orange	2204 Soft Orange
◈	43 Blue Violet	810 Blue Violet
◈	18 Deep Purple	8147 Deep Purple

	Dharma	PRO Chem
◈	28A Aqua Marine	7140 Aqua Marine
◈	93 Kilt Green	7218 Kilt Green
◈	6 Deep Orange	202 Strong Orange
◈	123 Fuchsia	308 Fuchsia

	Dharma	PRO Chem
◈	N/A	1203 Hollandaise
◈	64 Orchid	N/A
◈	14A Hot Pink	3142 Hot Pink
◈	N/A	731 Lemon/Lime

	Dharma	PRO Chem
◈	23 Cerulean Blue	406 Intense Blue
◈	6 Deep Orange	202 Strong Orange
◈	5 Soft Orange	2204 Soft Orange
◈	18A Ultraviolet	8194 Ultraviolet

	Dharma	PRO Chem
◈	10 Fire Red	310 N Basic Red
◈	31 Dark green	7207 Dark Green
◈	N/A	7158 Brightest Green
◈	19 Plum	8153 Plum

	Dharma	PRO Chem
◈	65 Raspberry	8136 Raspberry
◈	19 Plum	8153 Plum
◈	N/A	731 Lemon/Lime
◈	93 Kilt Green	7218 Kilt Green

Split Complements

Split complements are analogous colors with a complement chosen from across the wheel. They offer tension and resolution at the same time. These make the best toned, smoky, earthy browns. These colors either shine against each other as complements or to mix into earth tones. They also make a thermal shock color combination together for both thread and natural fabric recipes. Color an arc of analogous shades and pick a complementary of one of them for the center.

	Dharma	PRO Chem
♣	3A Clear Yellow	1229 Clear Yellow
♣	3 Golden Yellow	111 Mustard Yellow
♣	5 Soft Orange	2204 Soft Orange
♣	6 Deep Orange	202 Strong Orange
♣	9 Scarlet	300 Scarlet
♣	18 Deep Purple	8147 Deep Purple

	Dharma	PRO Chem
	3A Clear Yellow	1229 Clear Yellow
	19A Lilac	8199 Lilac
	19 Plum	8153 Plum
	18A Ultraviolet	8194 Ultraviolet
	43 Blue Violet	810 Blue Violet
	18 Deep Purple	8147 Deep Purple

	Dharma	PRO Chem
	65 Raspberry	8136 Raspberry
	19 Plum	8153 Plum
	13 Fuchsia	308 Fuchsia
	18 Deep Purple	8147 Deep Purple
	14A Hot Pink	3142 Hot Pink
	93 Kilt Green	7218 Kilt Green

	Dharma	PRO Chem
	6 Deep Orange	202 Strong Orange
	25 Turquoise	410 Turquoise
	106 Cayman Isle	7132 Cayman Isle
	132 Caribbean Blue	N/A
	23 Cerulean Blue	406 Intense Blue
	22 Cobalt Blue	402C Mixing Blue

The Natural World

natural color is the color we expect from the natural world. But expectation is really imagination, and of course, it falls flat. All color is a reflection of the light. The color is transformed as the light changes. Blue water can turn gray, green, lavender, purple, red and gold. The time of day effects the color. Sponge dyeing is perfect for creating the natural world, because of the riot of colors that echoes the complexity and richness of the natural world. Choose water colors that show what time of day it is.

Northern Lights	Dharma	PRO Chem
	13 Fuchsia	308 Fuchsia
	14A Hot Pink	3142 Hot Pink
	65 Raspberry	8136 Raspberry
	28A Aqua Marine	N/A
	106 Cayman Island	7132 Cayman Island
	19 Plum	8153 Plum
	21 Teal Blue	4222 Teal Blue

Tropical	Dharma	PRO Chem
	1 Lemon Yellow	114 Lemon Yellow
	N/A	731 Lemon/Lime
	92 Bright Green	7158 Bright Green
	28A Aqua Marine	7140 Aqua Marine
	50 Jade Green	7221 Jade Green
	19 Plum	8153 Plum
	28A Better Blue Green	N/A

Pond Scum	Dharma	PRO Chem
	3 Gold Yellow	111 Mustard Yellow
	3A Clear Yellow	1229 Clear Yellow
	32 Olive Drab	708N Olive Drab
	47 Chartreuse	706 Chartreuse
	18 Deep Purple	8147 Deep Purple
	31 Dark Green	7207 Dark Green
	93 Kilt Green	7218 Kilt Green

Sunrise Pastels	Dharma	PRO Chem
	N/A	1203 Hollandaise
	3A Clear Yellow	1229 Clear Yellow
	7A Peach	2139 Peach
	14A Hot Pink	3142 Hot Pink
	64 Orchid	N/A
	61 Ice Blue	4190 Ice Blue
	19A Lilac	8199 Lilac

Night Sky	Dharma	PRO Chem
	22 Cobalt Blue	Mixing Blue
	23 Cerulean Blue	406 Intense Blue
	24 Navy	412 Navy
	43 Blue Violet	810 Blue Violet
	27 Midnight Blue	414 Deep Navy

Grove	Dharma	PRO Chem
	1 Lemon Yellow	114 Lemon Yellow
	N/A	731 Lemon/Lime
	92 Bright Green	7158 Bright Green
	30A Emerald Green	704 Spring Green
	43 Blue Violet	810 Blue Violet

Lagoon	Dharma	PRO Chem
	1 Lemon Yellow	114 Lemon Yellow
	80 Robins Egg	4143 Robin Egg
	25 Turquoise	410 Turquoise
	132 Caribbean Blue	N/A
	28A Aqua Marine	7140 Aqua Marine
	23 Cerulean Blue	406 Intense Blue
	22 Cobalt Blue	402 Mixing Blue

Sunset	Dharma	PRO Chem
	3A Clear Yellow	1229 Clear Yellow
	5 Soft Orange	2204 Soft Orange
	6 Deep Orange	202 Strong Orange
	123 Fuchsia	308 Fuchsia
	9 Scarlet	300 Scarlet
	10 Fire Red	310 N Basic Red
	18A Ultraviolet	8194 Ultraviolet

Fall	Dharma	PRO Chem
	3A Clear Yellow	1229 Clear Yellow
	3 Golden Yellow	111 Mustard Yellow
	5 Soft Orange	2204 Soft Orange
	6 Deep Orange	202 Strong Orange
	9 Scarlet	300 Scarlet
	10 Fire Red	310 N Basic Red
	28A Better Blue Green	N/A

Lakes	Dharma	PRO Chem
	3A Clear Yellow	1229 Clear Yellow
	5 Soft Orange	2204 Soft Orange
	6 Deep Orange	202 Strong Orange
	106 Cayman Island Green	7132 Cayman Island Green
	132 Caribbean Blue	N/A
	23 Cerulean Blue	406 Intense Blue
	31 Dark green	7207 Dark Green

13

Dyeing Tools and Chemicals

MX Procion® dye is fiber reactive. It reacts with the fabric to form a chemical bond. It comes in a huge range of colors. It's extremely color fast and incredibly rich. Procion™ bonds best with plant fibers such as cotton, rayon, bamboo and hemp. They will not work on polyester, nylon, acrylic, or other synthetics at all.

A mask is a good idea while you're mixing or cleaning up dry dye. Wet dye is not hazardous.

Cotton fabric often comes with different coatings. Some wash off, some do not. Better to buy fabric that is PFD (prepared for dyeing). All kinds of cottons are available in many different weights. Fabrics with polyester content and resin coatings do not work well. Mercerized fabric has been treated so that the fibers are open to the dye and yield the richest colors I prefer P&B's bleached and mercerized dyer's muslin. You can also use rayon, flax and bamboo fabrics as well. But beware of anything that is crease resistant. If it resists creases, it resists dye.

Soda Ash is sodium carbonate. It's a mild alkali that acts as a catalyst for attaching the dye to the fabric. It's used in presoak and in pre-wash. It's also called washing soda, PH Up and Dye Activator.

Gloves come in latex, vinyl and nitrile. If you're allergic to latex, use one of the other kind. You'll need gloves even if you use Invisible Glove™.

Plastic cups for dye are essential. I use 4 oz. cups because it wastes less dye.

Urea is a wetting agent, available from dye houses and used in chemical water to mix dyes.

Bleach is the answer to most accidents. Don't let it near your fibers. Don't clean up with bleach until everything is in the bag.

Reduran™ is a more mild cleansing cream for hands and everything else personal that gets dyed. You need to apply it while your hands are dry for it to work

Paper Towels are essential for clean up and can be ironed afterwards and used as paper for art projects.

Sta-Flow™ is a liquid starch you can purchase at the grocery store. It adds body to fabric and can be diluted and sprayed on or put in the last rinse out.

Synthrapol™ is a chemical detergent and wetting agent made to remove dye and grease. It's used to pre-scrub fabric, as a wetting agent for chemical water, and to wash out dye.

Mil-Soft™ or Soft-Pro™ is a industrial softener. Small amounts will improve the hand of your fabric.

*Mangles were the household appliance of the forties. I can iron 50 yards of fabric in two hours with a mangle.

*Suction block™ sponges hold around 1 cup of water at a time. I use them to contain spills, one on each side of the table.

*Wringer Washers are a great appliance for holding soak water and for wringing out fabric.

*Invisible Glove™ is a cream that protects your skin from dye. You'll still want to wear your gloves but it helps you keep hands clean.

*Neat but not necessary things to have!

General Supplies

You'll need

- PFD Mercerized Fabric
- Small cups
- Yardstick
- Scissors
- Urea
- Synthrapol™
- Washing soda
- Cosmetic Sponges
- Clean up Sponges
- Newspaper
- Bleach
- Paper Towels
- Procion ™ dyes
- Plastic Zip-lock bags
- Clothes that you don't care about
- Buckets (I use a wringer washer)
- Mask
- Labels
- Gloves

Formulas

Soda Ash Soak

1 cup of soda ash for each gallon of water. Make sure to agitate the water when you put in the soda ash, so it dissolves. Soda ash water can be kept indefinitely as long as it's not contaminated with dye. I keep mine in a wringer washer that can be covered. Fabric needs to sit at least 10 minutes in soda ash to raise the chemical ph of the fabric and activate the dye.

Chemical Water for Mixing Dyes

Use ¼ cup of urea and a drop of Synthrapol™ to 1 quart of water.

Dye Solution

Use ⅓ of a cup of chemical water to 2-6 tablespoons of dye. Add dye powder to chemical water. Darker colors take more dye for truly strong hues. You can always add chemical water to dye cups as long as there's dye sediment in the bottom. Don't forget to wear your mask when you work with dry dye.

Preparing to Dye

  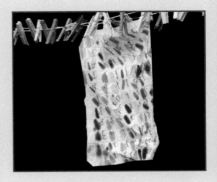

- Put on clothes you don't care about. Cover everything that matters with plastic and the floor with newspaper.
- Label the cups with the dye color. Mix your dye solutions as above and add a cosmetic sponge into each cup.
- Cut your fabric into lengths. I dye 1/2 yards, 1 yards and 1 1/2 yards usually. Soak the fabric for ten minutes in soda ash soak and wring it out. Sort your fabric by size so you know what size piece you're working with before you pick it up.
- You may want to make yourself a fabric dye chart. Printed charts are never as accurate. You don't need to wash it out, but you will want to label it.

Dyeing Fabric

You'll need
- Clean up Sponges
- Newspaper
- Bleach
- Paper Towels
- Gloves
- Mixed dye
- Chemical water
- Plastic Zip lock™ bags
- Clothes that you don't care about

Dyeing is a totally tactile experience. Rinse your hands before you dye each piece. Whatever is on your hands and the table will be instantly be on your fabric. Set up the cups of dye you want to use for your piece. Lay down a piece of fabric (I never stretch it flat or smooth because I like the textures) and start sponging the lightest colors first. Your dye is a bomb without a boom. It has a half life. It's connecting molecularly with the fabric. So if you dye the lighter colors first, they will remain light as you add darker ones around them because their molecules are already attached to the lighter dye and have no room for the next colors.

Add darker and darker colors until you reach the edges. I took my darkest purple and flicked dye on the center so it will be speckled. If I lift the fabric from the table, it will blur and blend more. I usually just swirl it and put it directly in the bag. You can sponge, draw, drip or squirt dye as you like. After all, it is your fabric. It needs to please you. I do find that the less I fuss or try to control it, the better the fabric is.

This method creates a variegated, striped fabric. Twist the fabric into a rope, vertically, horizontally or at a diagonal. Sponge on the first 2 or 3 lighter colors while it's twisted. Untwist it and add darker colors into the undyed areas. You can accentuate lighter colors in one area or create a general striped effect.

Once fabric is dyed it needs to go into a plastic bag and sit at least 12 hours. Use sandwich bags for ½ yards, quart bags for yards and gallon bags for 1-3 yard pieces. It needs to cure wet. At that point almost of the dye has connected to almost all of the fabric molecules and we say the dye is exhausted. Don't worry if you can't wash it for a while. Nothing grows in soda ash solution, so it won't mold or mildew. Separate out fabric that have reds in them. Reds are the only dye likely to bleed. They should be washed out separately from the other fabrics.

Fill up your washer with hot water. Add 3 small capfuls of Synthrapol ™. Wash again with Synthrapol™ and fill the softener cup of the washer with Sta-Flow Liquid Starch™. Add a teaspoon of Mil-Soft™ to the cup. When the cycle is finished your fabric is starched and softened. I let my fabric line dry and then I run it through my mangle, a rotary iron relic of the 1940's. The fabric is now starched, needle ready and beautiful.

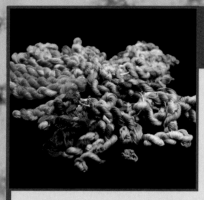

Dyeing Threads

You'll need
- Dye mixed in dye cups
- Wide plastic wrap
- Colander
- Mercerized cotton thread in dyers hanks
- Metal shower curtain hooks

Dyeing Threads
Untwist the threads and put them on metal shower curtain hooks to keep them from tangling. Soak the threads in soda ash soak, and drain them in a colander. Lay them out flat on the table. I usually use six colors per thread. I sponge dye on the threads, and cover that layer with plastic wrap. Then I lay the next layer of thread on top of that. When I'm all done, there are several layers of thread in plastic wrap, waiting to be washed out in 12 hours.

 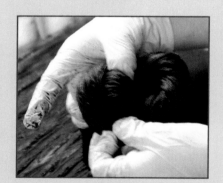 

Washing Out Threads
Lift the plastic off the first layer of threads. Put all the skeins from each layer on one finger, grab both ends and twist them (over the sponge to collect the drips). When they're tightly twisted, tuck one end into the other. Put the lump into the toe of a nylon knee high and knot the stocking. You can put three lumps in a queen-size knee high. Put knotted stockings into a nylon mesh bag and put them in the washer. Set the washer for its smallest load, hot water, and delicate fabrics. Put in one capful of Sythrapol™ and wash. Second wash, use one cap of Synthrapol™ and a capful of Mil-Soft™ into the softener cup. When the threads are washed out, carefully cut the stockings, untwist the thread, and de-tangle them. Put each thread grouping on a shower hook and it hang them up to dry.

18

Tips and Ellenisms on Dyeing

Hand-dye goes best with more hand-dye. So dye some more! It can be addictive. You've been warned. The good news is that it is not fattening. If you can, take notes on what colors you've used. That way you can keep track of combinations you particularly like and don't like.

- For best results, always use mercerized fabric and threads, prepared for dyeing.
- Always label your dye cups. You only think you know what color it is.
- Don't dye where you eat. Don't eat where you dye. Don't breathe in dye. Respect the chemicals.
- Printed dye charts are not exact. Make yourself a dye chart on fabric. You don't need to wash it out. Just hang it up where you can see it.
- Soak water lasts forever unless it's contaminated with dye. Change the water if you see a color cast to it.
- Dye your lightest colors first. The dye bonds with the fabric chemically. If it hits the fabric first, there's fewer places for the darker colors to attach to.
- Weigh fabric with darker or complementary colors at the bottom to give it depth.
- Use a suction block sponge on either side of your dye area to catch spills.
- Keep a bowl of water on the table to keep your hands clean and keep from contaminating dye or fabric.
- Line up your colors together as you're working on a piece to keep focused.
- When you are starting a new range of colors, clean the table thoroughly. Dye on the table is dye on your fabric.

- Keep your lighter colored sponges from being contaminated by holding the sponge in the palm of your hand and brushing the fabric with the back of your hand while squeezing the sponge.
- The more you handle your fabric the more indistinct it will become. Dye it and bag it promptly.
- Reds (especially fuchsia) bleed more than other colors. Wash reds separately to avoid them bleeding into other colors.
- You can add more chemical water to dye in the bottom of the cup as long as you have dye sludge in the cup. After that you're just diluting the dye.
- Dye remains active for 2 days and starts to weaken.
- Dye house chemicals are always more concentrated than grocery store ones.
- Dawn™ detergent is chemically close to Sythrapol™ and can be substituted in a pinch.
- Don't put your fabric in the dyer. Hang it up to damp dry and iron it.
- No piece of fabric is worth your fingers. Whatever is happening to your fabric in the iron or mangle, let it go until you can grab it safely.
- Of course you can cut into it. It only bleeds in the wash.

My Favorite Dyes

Primaries	☽♥	☽♥	☽♥	✺♥		✺♥
Dharma	1 Lemon Yellow	23 Cerulean Blue	11A Rose Red	2 Bright Yellow	22 Cobalt Blue	10 Fire Red
PRO Chem	114 Lemon Yellow	406 Intense Blue	305 Mixing Red	104 Golden Yellow	402C Mixing Blue	310 N Basic Red

Shade Colors	☽	☽♥	☽♥	☽♥	☽	☽
Dharma	97 Citrus	N/A	N/A	13 Fuchsia	7A Peach	11A Rose Red
PRO Chem	2021 Citrus	108 Sun Yellow	731 Lemon/Lime	308 Fuchsia	2139 Peach	305 Mixing Red

Shade	☽♥	☽♡	☽♥	☽♥	☽♥	☽♥
Dharma	61 Ice Blue	43 Blue Violet	19A Lilac	19 Plum	65 Raspberry	21 Teal Blue
PRO Chem	4190 Ice Blue	810 Blue Violet	8199 Lilac	8153 Plum	8136 Raspberry	4222 Teal Blue

Shade	☽♥	☽		☽♥	☽♥	☽♥
Dharma	23 Cerulean Blue	N/A	24 Navy	25 Turquoise	27 Midnight Blue	28A Aqua Marine
PRO Chem	406 Intense Blue	435 Marine	412 Navy	410 Turquoise	414 Deep Navy	7140 Aqua Marine

Shade	☽♥	☽♥	☽♥	☽♥	☽♥	☽♥
Dharma	106 Cayman Island Green	93 Kilt Green	132 Caribbean Blue	28A Better Blue Green	66 Kelly Green	92 Bright Green
PRO Chem	7132 Cayman Island Green	7218 Kilt Green	N/A	N/A	730 Lime	7158 Bright Green

Shade	✺♥	✺♥	✺♥	✺	✺♥	✺
Dharma	8 Rust Orange	3 Golden Yellow	3A Clear Yellow	4 Deep Yellow	5 Soft Orange	6 Deep Orange
PRO Chem	2215 Rust Orange	111 Mustard Yellow	1229 Clear Yellow	115 Butterscotch	2204 Soft Orange	202 Strong Orange

Sun	✺	✺♥	✺	✺♥	✺	
Dharma	312N Strongest Red	9 Scarlet	14 Coral Pink	14A Hot Pink	12A Baby Pink	95 Royal Blue
PRO Chem	49 Red Wine	300 Scarlet	332 Grecian Rose	3142 Hot Pink	N/A	400 Basic Blue

Sun	✹ ♥	✹	✹	✹	✹	✹
Dharma	18 Deep Purple	18A Ultraviolet	60 Lavender	64 Orchid	119 Red Violet	23A Electric Blue
PRO Chem	8147 Deep Purple	8194 Ultraviolet	8133 Lavender	N/A	N/A	404 Brightest Blue

Earth Colors	❄	❄	❄	❄	❄	❄
Dharma	111 Eggplant	47 Chartreuse	16 Maroon	33 Avocado	N/A	36A Havana Brown
PRO Chem	825 Eggplant	706 Chartreuse	3208 Maroon	7212 Avocado	435 Marine	5214 Havana Brown
Earth	❄	❄	❄	❄	❄	❄
Dharma	15 Burgundy	17 Amethyst	37 Bronze	Olive Drab	111 Black Cherry	N/A
PRO Chem	319 Bordeaux	8149 Amethyst	5193 Bronze	708N Olive	8131 Spicy Plum	7222 Balsam Fir

Sources

PRO Chemical and Dye ♥
http://www.prochemical.com/ 800-228-9393
Dyes, fabrics and wearables

The Cotton Club   www.cottonclub.com
1-208-345-5567
#5 DMC and Presencia Pearl Cotton

Dharma Trading Company ♥
www.dharmatrading.com
(800) 542-5227
Fabrics, wearables, tools and dyes

Test Fabrics www.testfabrics.com
PDF Fabrics and thread skeins
570-603- 0432

Glacier Quilts ♥ www.shopworks.com/
glacierquilts/Phone: 406-257-6966
P&B Dyers bleached mercerized Muslin
(my favorite) #5 DMC Pearl Cotton

Rupert, Gibbon & Spider, Inc.
www.jacqardproducts.com
800-442-0455
Procion™ dyes

Invisible Glove™ www.Amazon.com ♥
Sold by Auto Alley

White Wizard Products ♥
Suction Block Sponges™
http://www.whitewizardproducts.com/

Mangles and wringer washers sometimes show up in yard sales, on eBay, or on Craig's list. But your best bet is local. Ask older folk who are downsizing.

✹ Sun ☽ Shade ❄ Earth ♥ Favorites

CPSIA information can be obtained
at www.ICGtesting.com
Printed in the USA
274209LV00006B